Searchlight
BOOKS™

Do You
Know the
Continents?

Learning about Australia

Lisa Owings

Lerner Publications ◆ Minneapolis

Content Consultant: Kent Barnes, Associate Professor, Department of Geography and Environmental Planning, Towson University

Lerner Publications Company
A division of Lerner Publishing Group, Inc.
241 First Avenue North
Minneapolis, MN 55401 USA

For reading levels and more information, look up this title at www.lernerbooks.com.

Library of Congress Cataloging-in-Publication Data

Owings, Lisa.
    Learning about Australia / by Lisa Owings.
        pages cm. — (Searchlight books. Do you know the continents?)
    Includes index.
    Audience: Grades 4 to 6.
    ISBN 978-1-4677-8022-3 (lb : alk. paper) — ISBN 978-1-4677-8349-1
(pb : alk. paper) — ISBN 978-1-4677-8350-7 (eb pdf)
        1. Australia—Juvenile literature. I. Title.
    DU96.O95 2015
    994—dc23   2015001948

Manufactured in the United States of America
1 – VP – 7/15/15

Contents

Chapter 1

THE LAND DOWN UNDER

Welcome to the land down under! That is Australia's famous nickname. If you look at Australia on a globe, it is below most other continents. It is the only continent besides Antarctica that is fully south of the equator. It is also the only continent that is a country too.

Australia is home to unique landscapes and creatures. What is the continent's nickname?

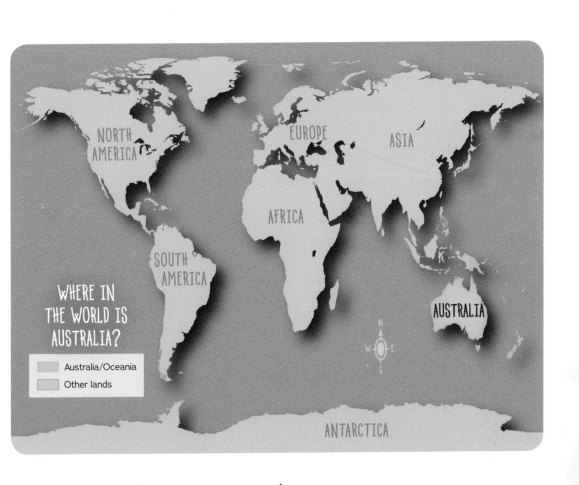

WHERE IN
THE WORLD IS
AUSTRALIA?

Australia/Oceania
Other lands

NORTH
AMERICA

EUROPE

ASIA

AFRICA

SOUTH
AMERICA

AUSTRALIA

ANTARCTICA

AUSTRALIA COVERS APPROXIMATELY
2.97 MILLION SQUARE MILES
(7.69 MILLION SQUARE KILOMETERS).

Surrounding Lands and Waters

Water surrounds Australia. The Indian Ocean curves around the western half of the continent. Pacific Ocean waves crash against the eastern half. On the northeast coast is the Great Barrier Reef. It is a huge system of colorful coral. Diverse plants and animals live there. The island of Tasmania sits southeast of Australia.

Most of Australia's people live near the continent's long coastline.

The amazing landscapes of New Zealand lie several hundred miles to Australia's southeast.

Seas separate Australia from its neighbors. Far to Australia's south is the frozen continent of Antarctica. The islands of Southeast Asia lie to the northwest. They include Indonesia and the Philippines.

Some people group Australia with nearby island nations. They combine the continent with New Zealand, New Guinea, and many small islands. Together, they call these places Oceania.

Exploring Australia

What do you think of when you think of Australia? Perhaps you picture jumping kangaroos and cuddly koalas. Maybe it's friendly people saying "g'day." Or you might think of the remote areas known as the outback. Australia has all this and more.

Australia's outback extends across the continent's center.

IN ADDITION TO ITS STUNNING LANDSCAPES, AUSTRALIA HAS LARGE CITIES.

Australia is the smallest continent. It is about as big as the United States. Yet it has many varied places to explore. The continent has native villages and huge cities. It has lush rain forests and dry deserts. It also has plants and animals found nowhere else on Earth. People from around the world come to see the land down under.

Chapter 2

STATES AND CITIES

Australia's first people are known as the Aboriginal people. Scientists have found evidence suggesting they arrived on the continent about 60,000 years ago. The Aboriginal people traveled from Asia by boat. They quickly spread across Australia.

Australia's early Aboriginal settlers left behind artwork on rocks. How did they travel to Australia?

Large numbers of European people first arrived in Australia in the late 1700s. British explorer James Cook claimed the continent for Great Britain. Europeans soon forced the Aboriginal people off their lands.

Europeans continued to come to Australia in the 1800s. They formed six colonies on the continent. The colonies joined together in 1901. They became the Commonwealth of Australia.

James Cook also explored New Zealand and Hawaii.

Western Australia has many rocky landscapes.

Australian States

Modern Australia is made up of states and territories. States can pass their own laws. Territories need the national government's permission to pass laws.

Western Australia is the largest state. The state of Queensland sits on Australia's northeastern corner. New South Wales and Victoria lie along the southeastern coast. South Australia is in the lower middle of Australia. The island state of Tasmania is in the southeast.

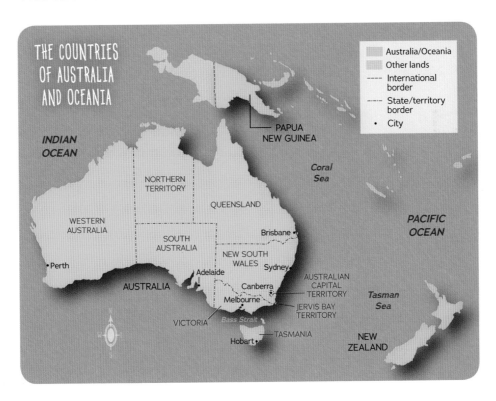

THE COUNTRIES OF AUSTRALIA AND OCEANIA

	Australia/Oceania
	Other lands
----	International border
----	State/territory border
•	City

INDIAN OCEAN

PAPUA NEW GUINEA

Coral Sea

NORTHERN TERRITORY

QUEENSLAND

WESTERN AUSTRALIA

SOUTH AUSTRALIA

Brisbane

NEW SOUTH WALES

Sydney

PACIFIC OCEAN

Perth

AUSTRALIA

Adelaide

Canberra

AUSTRALIAN CAPITAL TERRITORY

Melbourne

JERVIS BAY TERRITORY

Tasman Sea

VICTORIA

Bass Strait

TASMANIA

NEW ZEALAND

Hobart

WHERE ARE AUSTRALIA'S LARGE CITIES LOCATED? WHY MIGHT THIS BE?

Three of Australia's territories are on the mainland. The Northern Territory covers north-central Australia. The Australian Capital Territory is in southeast Australia. It includes the capital city, Canberra. On the coast near Canberra is the Jervis Bay Territory. Other territories are small islands near the continent. One territory is in Antarctica. Australian scientists work there. They study the continent.

Canberra is home to the Parliament House, where Australia's lawmakers work.

The Sydney Opera House attracts tourists from around the world.

Australia's government is based in Canberra. But most Australians live in other major cities. Sydney is the largest. It is the state capital of New South Wales. About 4.5 million people live there. The city is known for its famous opera house. Other major cities include Melbourne and Brisbane. Both are on the east coast. Perth is on the west coast. It is the capital of Western Australia.

Chapter 3

LANDFORMS AND CLIMATE

Dry plains cover most of Australia. About one-third of the continent's land is desert. Temperatures here rise above 100°F (38°C) in the summer. Grasses and brittle shrubs cover another third of the continent. The rest has a mix of mountains, forests, and beaches.

Shrubs and grasses can survive in dry areas. How much of Australia is covered in these plants?

Mountains and Rivers

Australia's mountains rise along its Pacific coast. The biggest group is the Great Dividing Range. The southern peaks are capped in snow during the winter.

The Murray River flows from the Great Dividing Range. It is one of Australia's few permanent rivers. Most of the continent's rivers are dry for part of the year.

The Murray River flows west and drains into the Indian Ocean.

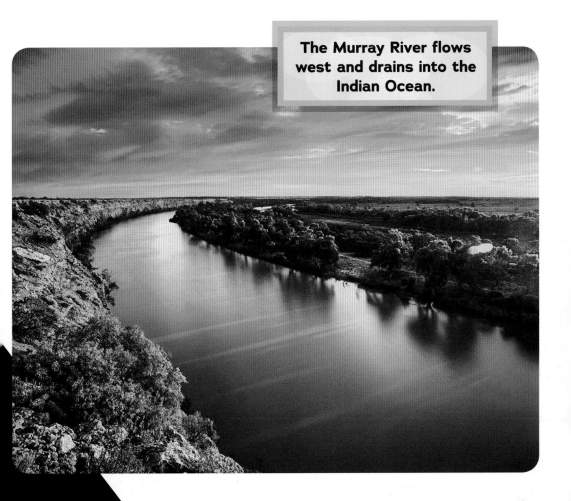

Many of Australia's rain forests have rivers and waterfalls.

Rain Forests and Deserts

Rain forests are found in northern Queensland. The climate here is tropical. It gets much more rain than central Australia. Some parts get more than 40 inches (102 centimeters) of rain each year. Grasslands fill central Australia. The western half of the continent is mostly desert. Sand blows across the landscape. The wind shapes the sand into tall dunes.

WHAT IS THE MOST COMMON CLIMATE ZONE IN AUSTRALIA?

▼

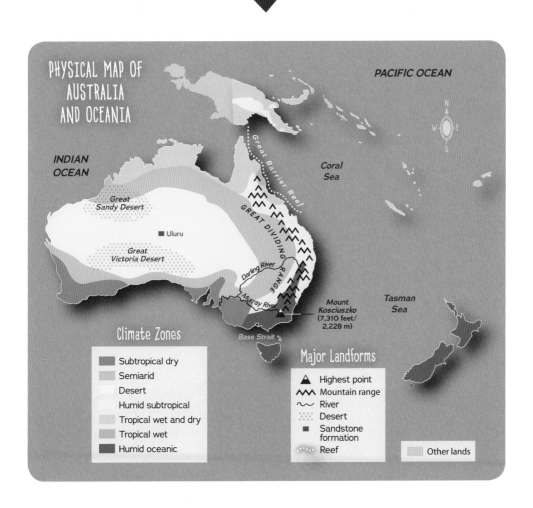

PHYSICAL MAP OF
AUSTRALIA
AND OCEANIA

PACIFIC OCEAN

INDIAN
OCEAN

Coral
Sea

Great Barrier Reef

Great
Sandy Desert

GREAT DIVIDING RANGE

■ Uluru

Great
Victoria Desert

Darling River

Murray River

Tasman
Sea

Mount
Kosciuszko
(7,310 feet/
2,228 m)

Bass Strait

Climate Zones

- Subtropical dry
- Semiarid
- Desert
- Humid subtropical
- Tropical wet and dry
- Tropical wet
- Humid oceanic

Major Landforms

- ▲ Highest point
- ⋀⋀ Mountain range
- ∿ River
- ⋯ Desert
- ■ Sandstone formation
- ⋯ Reef

Other lands

One of Australia's most famous features is a huge red rock called Uluru. It is in the desert of the Northern Territory. The rock stands more than 1,000 feet (305 meters) tall and is about 5.8 miles (9.3 kilometers) around! It is also known as Ayers Rock. The rock is sacred to the Aboriginal people.

Seasons in Australia

The seasons in Australia are the opposite of those in the Northern Hemisphere. Summers in Australia are December to February. Winters last from June to August. Australian summers are mostly hot and dry. Winters are usually mild. Frost and snow are found only in Australia's southern areas.

ULURU IS THE ROCK'S ABORIGINAL NAME. EUROPEAN SETTLERS CALLED IT AYERS ROCK.

The Great Barrier Reef

The Great Barrier Reef lies off Australia's northeastern coast. But it is more than just one reef. There are thousands! Put together, they are the size of Japan. They can even be seen from space. The coral reefs are filled with life. Fish swim among corals, anemones, and urchins. Turtles and whales come to feed. Seaweed and algae grow on the colorful reefs.

Chapter 4

NATURAL RESOURCES

Many Australian plants and animals are found nowhere else on Earth. Tree kangaroos and ringtail possums live in the rain forest. Vines, ferns, and orchids cover the trees.

The ringtail possum lives in eastern Australia's forests. What other animals live in the continent's forests?

Birds and butterflies add color to the forest. Huge birds known as cassowaries have blue heads. They cannot fly. Instead, they walk along the forest floor. Male golden bowerbirds build huge nests to attract mates. The Ulysses butterfly has neon blue wings.

Southern and eastern Australia have cooler, dryer forests. Eucalyptus trees are common. Koalas feed on their leaves. Other animals here include gray kangaroos and wombats. Cockatoos and kookaburras perch in the trees.

The kangaroo is one of Australia's most famous animals.

Australians often call acacia trees *wattles*.

Life in the Desert

Life survives even in the heat of Australia's deserts. Flowery acacia trees take root. During dry times, acacia trees stop growing. They can survive until the next rain comes. The shape of their branches sends water to the ground around the trunk. This gives the tree as much water as possible.

Red kangaroos and emus race across the plains. Packs of wild dogs called dingoes hunt smaller animals. The outback is also home to lizards and snakes. Snakes called taipans and death adders have deadly bites. Many of the planet's deadliest snakes live in Australia.

Weird and Wonderful Mammals

Many of the world's marsupials are found in Australia. These mammals have pouches on their bodies to let them carry their young. Kangaroos and koalas are marsupials.

Monotremes are another kind of Australian mammal. Unlike other mammals, they lay eggs! Echidnas and platypuses are the only monotremes. Echidnas are spiny. They live in sheltered areas, such as caves. Platypuses have webbed feet. Their flat snouts look like duck bills.

Chapter 5

PEOPLE AND CULTURES

About 22.5 million people live in Australia. They are nicknamed Aussies. Almost all of them live in large cities near the coast. Few people live in the continent's harsh deserts.

Melbourne is one of Australia's largest cities. It has more than 4 million people. About how many people live on the continent in all?

Aussies are known for their friendly attitudes. Most of them have British or Irish ancestors. However, a growing number of Aussies are from Asia. Only about 1 percent of Australians are Aboriginal.

MANY OF AUSTRALIA'S PEOPLE
COME FROM EUROPE AND ASIA.

Popular Dishes

Meat and vegetables make up most Australian meals. In good weather, Aussies light up barbecues. They enjoy grilling their food. Asian dishes such as stir-fry and sushi are also popular. A yeast paste called Vegemite is spread on toast.

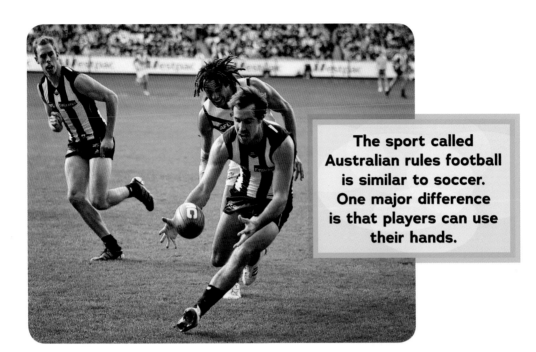

The sport called Australian rules football is similar to soccer. One major difference is that players can use their hands.

Daily Life

English is the official language in Australia. One-fourth of Aussies speak other languages. These include Asian, European, and Aboriginal languages.

Australia's large cities are full of skyscrapers and shopping centers. Life there is similar to life in the United States. People spend time at the beach. They go to the movies. They go on nature hikes. They watch and play sports. One popular sport is called Australian rules football. People also go to festivals for music and art. These events celebrate Australia's diverse people and cultures.

Some people live in the outback. They are often farmers or miners. Others live in Aboriginal communities. There are few modern roads in the outback. This can make travel difficult. The people of the outback help one another survive in these harsh areas.

▲

FARMERS IN THE OUTBACK RAISE CATTLE, SHEEP, AND OTHER ANIMALS.

Dreaming the World

In traditional Aboriginal beliefs, everything is connected to the spirit world. These beliefs hold that ancient beings created all things on Earth. People with these beliefs think the creation happened during a dreamtime. They say this creation is ongoing. Aboriginal people believe that dreamtime links the past and present. They sometimes perform traditional rituals and dances linked to these beliefs.

Chapter 6

ECONOMICS

Australia has one of the world's strongest economies. The continent is rich with a wide variety of natural resources. Some Australians find jobs involving these resources. Others find jobs in schools, shops, or with the government.

A huge gold mine is located in Western Australia. Besides mining, what other kinds of jobs do Australians have?

Mining and Energy

Mining is a major industry in Australia. Workers dig for minerals and gemstones. They find gold, diamonds, and iron ore. The eastern coast holds shiny opals and sapphires.

Energy is another important Australian resource. Fossil fuels provide much of Australia's energy. Companies find oil and natural gas off the coast. Queensland has many coal mines. Australia exports more coal than any other country. Dams in eastern Australia turn the rivers' energy into electricity.

Wivenhoe Dam is on the Brisbane River. It helps generate electricity for the area.

Farming

Australia produces nearly all the food it needs. The work of Australian farmers makes this possible. Most farmers raise animals. Sheep and cattle graze on the dry grasses. Farmers sell their meat and wool to other countries. Some land is watered and fertilized for crops. Australian farms produce wheat, sugar, and fruit.

Australia is one of the world's top wool-producing countries.

WHY MIGHT SHEEP FARMING BE MORE COMMON IN AUSTRALIA'S EASTERN AREAS THAN IN ITS CENTER?

▼

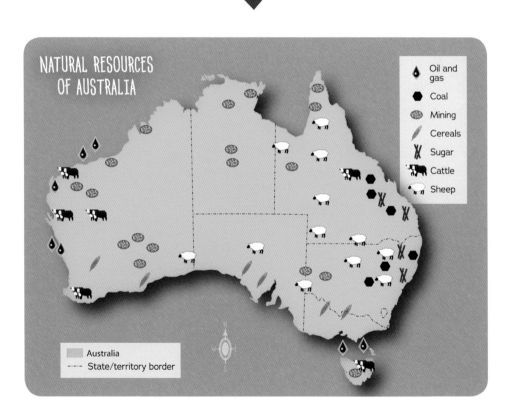

NATURAL RESOURCES OF AUSTRALIA

Oil and gas

Coal

Mining

Cereals

Sugar

Cattle

Sheep

Australia

State/territory border

Australian Jobs

Three-fourths of Australians work in the service industries. They provide services to the public. Teachers, doctors, and bankers are in service industries. So are workers in shops and in the government.

Wonders Down Under

Australia is filled with natural resources. It has a rich Aboriginal tradition. There are snowy mountains, hot deserts, and steamy rain forests. Nowhere in the world is quite like Australia. Where will your adventure down under begin?

Australia's amazing landscapes, cities, and animals make it an exciting continent to visit.

Exploring Australia

Choose two or three places from the maps in this book that you want to know more about. Pick places from different parts of Australia. Research these places online. What unique things are there to see and do? What do people eat? What local celebrations or festivals take place there? Write a paragraph about a trip that you will take to each place. What will you see and do?

Glossary

colony: a group of people living in a new area but still connected to their home country

commonwealth: a country that is ruled by its people

coral reef: a reef made of the hard skeletons of tiny sea creatures called corals

dam: a barrier across a river that holds back water

diverse: having many different types or backgrounds

dune: a hill of sand

fertilize: to apply chemicals to soil to make it richer

harsh: rough or cruel

hemisphere: half of planet Earth

mainland: the largest part of a country or continent

marsupial: an animal that carries its young in a pouch on the mother's belly

outback: an unsettled area of land far away from cities

permanent: lasting for a long time or forever

sacred: holy or very important

territory: an area of land that is ruled by a government

tropical: related to the hot, rainy area around the equator

Learn More about Australia

Books

Friedman, Mel. *Australia and Oceania*. New York: Children's Press, 2009. Learn more about Australia and its neighboring nations.

Wignell, Edel. *Bilby: Secrets of an Australian Marsupial*. Somerville, MA: Candlewick Press, 2015. Meet the bilby, an endangered marsupial that lives in Australia.

Wojahn, Rebecca Hogue, and Donald Wojahn. *An Australian Outback Food Chain*. Minneapolis: Lerner Publications, 2009. Learn about the wildlife in the Australian outback and how these creatures are all connected.

Websites

Kids Do Ecology: Coral Reef
http://kids.nceas.ucsb.edu/biomes/coralreef.html
Learn about the coral reefs that surround Australia and the animals and plants that inhabit them.

National Geographic Kids: Australia
http://kids.nationalgeographic.com/content/kids/en_US/explore/countries/australia
See the Australian flag, check out photos of the continent, and read more fast facts about Australia.

San Diego Zoo: Marsupials
http://animals.sandiegozoo.org/animals/marsupial
Find out more about marsupials in Australia.

Index

Photo Acknowledgments

The images in this book are used with the permission of: © tomograf/iStockphoto, p. 4; © Laura Westlund/Independent Picture Service, pp. 5, 13, 19, 35, 37; © wx-bradwang/iStockphoto, p. 6; © Lars Peter Lundstroem/iStockphoto, p. 7; © JurgaR/iStockphoto, p. 8; © NilsBV/iStockphoto, p. 9; © pamspix/iStockphoto, p. 10; © GeorgiosArt/iStockphoto, p. 11; © Anna Morgan/Shutterstock Images, p. 12; © Dan Breckwoldt/Shutterstock Images, p. 14; © ToolX/iStockphoto, p. 15; © Edward Haylan/Shutterstock Images, p. 16; © Ben Goode/iStockphoto, p. 17; © Susan Steward/iStockphoto, p. 18; © Stanislav Fosenbauer/Shutterstock Images, p. 20; © pniesen/iStockphoto, p. 21; © Monkeystock/Shutterstock Images, p. 22; © CraigRJD/iStockphoto, p. 23; © photosbyash/iStockphoto, p. 24; © Juniors Bildarchiv/Glow Images, p. 25; © George Clerk/iStockphoto, p. 26; © GTS Productions/Shutterstock Images, p. 27; © mirjana ristic damjanovic/Shutterstock Images, p. 28; © Neale Cousland/Shutterstock Images, p. 29; © Anne Greenwood/Shutterstock Images, p. 30; © Rick Rycroft/AP Images, p. 31; © Imagevixen/Shutterstock Images, p. 32; © covenant/Shutterstock Images, p. 33; © Baronb/Shutterstock Images, p. 34; © FiledImage/Shutterstock Images, p. 36.

Front Cover: © Universal History Archive/Getty Images.

Main body text set in Adrianna Regular 14/20.
Typeface provided by Chank.